★★★★★ DOUGLAS ★★★★★

MACARTHUR

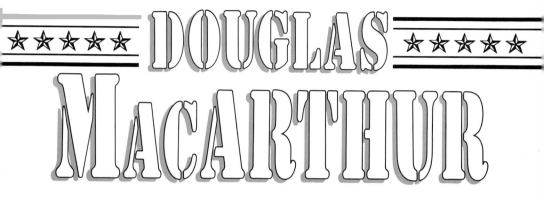

DOUGLAS MACARTHUR

Jean Darby

Lerner Publications Company • Minneapolis

Front and back cover photographs courtesy of the MacArthur Memorial

LIBRARY OF CONGRESS CATALOGING-IN-PUBLICATION DATA

Darby, Jean
    Douglas MacArthur / by Jean Darby.
        p.   cm.
    Bibliography: p.
    Includes index.
    Summary: A biography of the controversial military leader remembered for his defense of the Philippines during World War II, administration of occupied Japan after the war, and leadership of United Nations troops in the Korean conflict.
    ISBN 0-8225-4901-8 (lib. bdg.)
    1. MacArthur, Douglas, 1880-1964 — Juvenile literature.
2. Generals — United States — Biography — Juvenile literature.
3. United States — Army — Biography — Juvenile literature. 4. United States — History, Military — 20th century — Juvenile literature. [1. MacArthur, Douglas, 1880-1964. 2. Generals.] I. Title.
E745.M3D37   1989
355'.0092'4 — dc19
[B]
[92]   88-38405
                                                CIP
                                                 AC

Manufactured in the United States of America

2 3 4 5 6 7 8 9 10 98 97 96 95 94 93 92 91 90

Contents

Maps appear on pages 28, 58, 74-75, and 94.

Douglas MacArthur, commander in chief of the Southwest Pacific during World War II, with his favorite corncob pipe

∽ ONE ∽

Call of the Bugle

"My first recollection is that of a bugle call."
—Douglas MacArthur

The wind blew and the sun blazed down on whinnying horses, on rumbling wagons, and on the tired marchers of Company K. The 300-mile journey from Fort Wingate to Fort Selden led them across barren New Mexico land. In spite of thirst, dust, and sore feet, a four-year-old boy marched at the front of the troop. His name was Douglas MacArthur.

Commanding the troop was Douglas's father, Captain Arthur MacArthur. He was ambitious and determined that his young sons follow in his footsteps. On this day, however, he spoke gently to his horse and scanned the horizon for unfriendly Apaches. In one of the wagons rode Douglas's older brother, Arthur, and his mother, Mary Pinkney MacArthur, known as "Pinky."

With dust in their nostrils and the sun baking their heads, the troops turned their horses and wagons south and followed the east side of the Rio Grande River. Houses were scarce—small dots against the horizon or behind scraggly trees. Water was at a premium. At one place the troops came upon a lone rancher. "How far to the next water hole?" a member of the troop called.

The rancher cupped his hands around his mouth and, above the thudding of horse's hooves, shouted, "About 10 miles."

It was difficult to know distances in those days because there were no signs along the trail. After three hours of riding, they met another homesteader and asked again, "How far to the next water hole?"

The homesteader pulled his beard, then, as he scratched around under his hat he said, "I reckon about 10 miles."

Captain MacArthur knew that one of the homesteaders was wrong, but the troops had no choice. They had to travel on wondering if the water hole was 10 miles away, or if there was a water hole at all.

Finally they spotted a clump of trees on the horizon. The mounts quickened their pace. Leaning forward, the riders stared anxiously into the distance. Green grass! Cheers went up. They had found water. The soldiers drank and washed their faces. They filled their water barrels and canvas bags. They cooled their horses, then on they went.

Eventually they reached a small group of adobe houses nestled behind a high wall. With flags waving, and trumpets blaring, Company K entered through a gate and passed a crooked sign that read "Fort Selden."

Captain MacArthur gave the order, "Company halt."

Pinky and Arthur hustled out of the wagon. Douglas scurried about the courtyard investigating barred windows, big black pots, and the soft, warm noses of spotted ponies.

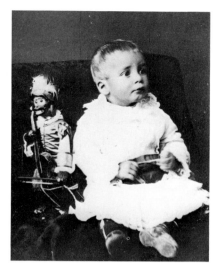

Douglas, top left, *at age 2, with a toy monkey at Fort Wingate; Mary Pinkney MacArthur,* bottom left, *his mother; Arthur MacArthur,* bottom right, *his father*

Soldiers and their wives greeted the new arrivals on the drill ground where the men usually practiced marching and other skills. The wagons were unloaded and Pinky stood with her hands on her hips staring into the small, square rooms that she was to make into a home. The task seemed impossible, but Pinky was a woman who did not give up easily. Quickly she set to work sweeping the floors and arranging furniture that was tattered and used. Even as she cleaned, though, dust from the drill ground crept into every nook.

"It will be all right," she told herself. "We'll manage."

Pinky was determined that her boys would receive an education. Because there was no school for them to attend, she became their teacher. In the 1880s, there were no lessons that could come through the mail, so she created her own program. Foremost in her mind was the sort of person she wanted her boys to become. Because of this, she stressed the moral principles she had learned from the Bible. "Always be honest," she told her boys. And because Pinky dreamed of her sons growing to be successful men, she told them, "I want you to be like your father or like Robert E. Lee." Although they'd fought on opposite sides during the Civil War, both men had fought well. She also reminded the boys that their country must always come first.

She found it easy to guide the boys' reading because books were scarce at the fort. There were no libraries and no stores where they could purchase dime novels or magazines. "You will learn to read in these," she said, as she handed them books about war heroes. No doubt this early reading influenced both boys' decisions to serve in the military.

With no running water, electricity, or coolers, life in the West was difficult, but for young boys it was often exciting. Cavalrymen came from other forts bringing tales of battles against Geronimo and the Apaches. The boys heard about desperadoes, murderers, and robbers who lived along the banks of the Rio Grande. They heard about William Bonney, alias "Billy the Kid," who terrorized New Mexico.

Douglas and Arthur loaded their rifles and prodded their ponies to go faster across the plains. Shirtless and shoeless, wearing headbands and leggings of tanned hide, they shot at rabbits that darted for shelter.

Inside the fort were the ever-present sounds of hooves, trumpets, and booming field guns. The smells were always those of animals, dust, and cooking.

At the end of each day Arthur and Douglas stood rigidly at attention during retreat ceremonies, eyes forward, hearts pounding.

∾

The exciting years at Fort Selden ended in 1886, after Douglas's sixth birthday, when his father announced the move to Fort Leavenworth, Kansas. There Douglas went to school for the first time. It was an unhappy day for him when he entered second grade. Sitting in school with several other children was different from the freedom he had known in the West and he missed his mother being the teacher. But Leavenworth did offer something special: cavalry on splendid mounts, artillery with long-barreled guns, and the infantry with its blaze of glittering bayonets. To Douglas, these sights were a never-ending thrill.

After Leavenworth came another change. In 1889, Douglas's father was transferred to Washington, D.C. For the first time, the MacArthurs lived in a city—a city with bright lights and parties, politicians and diplomats. But living in the nation's capitol did not offer the excitement of the early West.

Douglas finished the eighth grade with many stresses in his life. He started wearing glasses, and his mother made a plaid suit which he had to wear to school. How different from Fort Selden, where he could go without shirt or shoes! How different this was from the days when he could gallop his pony across vacant land.

The MacArthurs stayed in Washington for four years. Then, in 1893, they moved to Fort Sam Houston in Texas. Douglas was thrilled. Once again he was at a military post. He was fascinated with its activities but soon became even more excited with a school that was nearby, a military academy. "I want to go there," he told his parents.

Since his parents were ambitious for their sons, and because they wanted their children to follow in Captain MacArthur's footsteps, they were delighted. Arthur was already attending the U.S. Naval Academy in Annapolis, Maryland. Now Douglas entered the Texas Military Academy. School started at 8:25 A.M. and ended at 5:55 P.M.

As Douglas worked diligently and climbed to the head of his class, other cadets began to recognize his ability. Excelling scholastically, he also proved to be outstanding in athletics. He won the school tennis championship. He played shortstop on the baseball team and was quarterback on the football team. Best of all, he was promoted to first sergeant of his company. He also organized an elite drill unit that staged exhibitions at other schools throughout the territory.

When Douglas graduated in 1897, he was awarded the coveted gold medal for the highest standing in scholarship.

Still wanting to be as great as his father, he turned his thinking to an even higher goal: the United States Military Academy at West Point.

The MacArthur family poses at Fort Leavenworth, Kansas, in 1886. From left to right: Douglas; his father, Arthur; his brother, Arthur; his mother, "Pinky"

Douglas MacArthur excelled at sports when he attended West Texas Military Academy, his high school. He is the young man with number 96 on his jersey.

On campsite at Fort Sam Houston in Texas, F Battery practices military drills.

In October, 1897, Douglas and his mother moved to Congressman Theabold Otjen's district in Milwaukee, Wisconsin, about 300 miles from St. Paul, Minnesota, where his father had been sent. "The congressman was a friend of your grandfather's," Pinky explained. "He will appoint you to West Point." At least, that was what his mother hoped. But first Douglas needed to have a spinal defect corrected by a famous Milwaukee doctor so he could pass the West Point physical exam.

Douglas also had to prepare for competitive exams. Pinky hired a tutor from West End High. Every day for a year, Douglas walked two miles from their hotel to the school. He had never worked so hard in his life.

The night before the examination, he couldn't sleep. After breakfast, he was nauseated. His mother went with him to City Hall and on the steps she gave him a pep talk. "Doug," she said, "you'll win if you don't lose your nerve."

The *Milwaukee Journal* of June 7, 1898 told the story. Under the headline HE WILL GO TO WEST POINT, the paper reported that he had placed first.

✑ TWO ✑

A Soldier's Life

"Next to my family, I loved West Point best."
—Douglas MacArthur

In 1898, Douglas MacArthur's father was promoted to brigadier general. He then sailed to the Philippines, where he would be named military governor of Manila. One year later, on Tuesday, June 13, 1899, a West Shore Railroad train screeched to a stop and out stepped Douglas MacArthur and his mother. They walked up a steep hill and through a stone arch, until they stood before the U.S. Military Academy at West Point, New York. They saw the tall granite buildings, winding Flirtation Walk, and the walls that enclosed the cadet barracks.

"You'll be a great soldier," Pinky said. Then she picked up her luggage and followed the path down to the Hudson River where a yellow brick building called the Craney Hotel stood. Pinky would live here while her son attended West Point.

In the meantime, Douglas unpacked his clothes and

settled in Beast Barracks. "Here I am at West Point," he said to himself. "I passed the examinations. I received my appointment." At that time he did not realize how difficult his first few weeks would be.

Because of his father, who was becoming famous for his work in the Philippines, and because he was dubbed a "mother's boy," Douglas was hazed (teased and intimidated) unmercifully by the upperclassmen. He had to make funny speeches. Again and again he had to recite his father's military record. One time he was told to dress in full uniform, don a raincoat, and wrap himself in blankets. Covered so he could hardly move, he was then forced to sit through a hot night inside a tent. His treatment was severe, but he had been taught to be brave. First classman Robert E. Wood said of MacArthur, "All upperclassmen watched him for signs of weakness, but he came through with flying colors."

There were 332 cadets at the academy. They lived by strict rules and spoke their own language. Freshman were called "plebes;" sophomores, "yearlings;" juniors, "second classmen;" and seniors, "first classmen." The leader of the corps was "first captain." When a cadet called, "Hey, wife," he was calling to his roommate. When a cadet said, "She's my drag," he was saying the girl was his date. A demerit was a "quill" because it was written with a quill pen. "Ketchup" was "growly;" cream, "calf;" milk, "cow." Because an officer named Samuel Miles thought that bread and molasses were a healthy diet for cadets, molasses became "Sammy."

The cadets studied mathematics, history, and law. They also studied military engineering, geography, chemistry, minerals, matter, and energy. They were taught English grammar as well as Spanish and French. Because the students were training to be soldiers, they practiced gunnery and

This view of West Point Military Academy shows the plain, the barracks, and the West Academic Building in the early 1900s. Cadets learn both academic and military skills there.

military drills as well. Douglas often hit a bull's-eye at target practice, and he received excellent grades. In fact, he graduated first in his class.

At graduation in 1903, Second Lieutenant Douglas MacArthur pinned gold bars on his uniform and looked at himself in the mirror. Although he was pleased with his commission, he was already thinking about changing the gold bars to silver. With a smile, he wondered how long it would be until he moved up to first lieutenant.

Soon Douglas received his first military posting. His first orders sent him to the Philippines where his father had gained the love of its people. By this time, General Arthur MacArthur had returned home, and the Filipinos were at peace.

*Second Lieutenant
Douglas MacArthur
between 1903 and
1905, early in his
military career*

Douglas arrived in Manila late in October, 1903, after five weeks at sea. He stepped from the ship, breathed the sweet sea air, and looked at the mountains with their jagged peaks. With his hands on his hips, he gazed across the bay to Corregidor Island. MacArthur was already in love with the country. His passion for this part of the world aided him later when he was asked to defend it with marching men, ships, and artillery.

But that duty was in the future. Now he had other tasks to perform. As a young man of 23 he was an engineer assigned to the third battalion. He had come to the Philippines to supervise construction of a dock, to work on surveys, and to lead patrols.

Once he was sent into the jungle where two guerrillas attacked him. One of the guerrillas raised an old rifle and pulled the trigger. A slug tore through MacArthur's campaign hat. One more shot could have killed him. But MacArthur, quick with his pistol, drew his gun and shot both guerrillas.

His stay in the Philippines ended on October 4, 1904, when he sailed for San Francisco. During the next few months, he studied engineering and became a first lieutenant. It was a happy day when he took off his gold bars and replaced them with silver.

One day a telegram came. Quickly he ripped it open and read:

Special Order　　　　　　　War Department
No.222　　　　　　　　　　Washington, D.C.
　　　　　　　　　　　　　October 3, 1905

First Lieutenant Douglas MacArthur, corps of engineers, is relieved from present duties, and will proceed to Tokyo, Japan, and report in person to Major General Arthur MacArthur, U.S.A., for an appointment as aide-de-camp on his staff.

By Order Secretary of War

　　　　　　　J. C. Bates,
　　　　　　　Major General,
　　　　　　　Acting Chief of Staff

Douglas met his parents in Yokohama's Oriental Palace Hotel. A few days later they began their tour of Asia.

The three of them checked Japanese military bases, then sailed for Shanghai, Hong Kong, and Java. They celebrated Christmas in Singapore and New Year's Day in Burma. By January they were in India, where they spent two months inspecting several locations. In his topee (a lightweight helmet to protect his head from the sun) and white linen suit, Douglas was the picture of how a young American soldier should look. Underneath this handsome outer covering was a warm, sensitive man. Seeing people who were hungry made him unhappy. It bothered him to find so many families huddled in tiny shacks. Through the years, he never forgot the people of Asia.

When he returned to the United States in 1906, Douglas was disappointed by his assignment to an engineering school known as Washington Barracks. He had hoped to be assigned to a fort, and his studies did not go well.

"What about MacArthur?" an instructor asked. "I thought he was a fine student, but he is not."

Other instructors shook their heads. "Unpredictable," they said. "His work is not equal to that of other students. Is he lazy? Why doesn't he study the way he did at West Point?" His time at Washington Barracks left a bad mark on his record.

When he returned to Milwaukee in 1907, his life became even more complicated. His father had retired and wished his son to spend time with him. His mother wanted him to escort her to social functions. Torn between the army and his parents, he frequently suffered from an upset stomach. As pressures grew, he became more frustrated and unhappy. One day he couldn't stand it any longer and he talked back to a superior officer. Because this is inexcusable for military personnel, the officer wrote an efficiency report that gave MacArthur a poor rating. It said that MacArthur's duties were not performed in a satisfactory manner. This put another demerit on his record.

Pinky was furious. "They're being unfair," she snapped. She wanted to help her son get a civilian job so she wrote a letter to the owner of a railroad.

My Dear Mr. Harriman:

At Ambassador Griscom's in Tokyo some three years ago, I had the good fortune to be seated next to you at luncheon. The amiable manner in which you then listened to my talk, in behalf of a possible future for my son Douglas MacArthur outside the army, encourages me to address you now. As I recall you said that first class men are always in demand, and that you frequently have occasion to seek them. . . .

The letter went on to ask Mr. Harriman to find a place for Douglas with his company. As it turned out, Pinky's first mistake was writing the letter. Her second mistake was not telling Douglas what she had done. When a representative of the railroad came to interview Douglas, he was shocked. By then MacArthur had been transferred to Leavenworth. He had no intention of leaving the army.

On September 5, 1912, his father died. Since his brother, Arthur, had graduated from the U.S. Naval Academy and was currently serving on a ship at sea, Douglas assumed responsibility for his mother. Pinky moved to Leavenworth.

Douglas was happy to be back in a fort—back where he felt he belonged. Assigned the lowest ranked of 22 companies, he began to work on ways to bring it up to standard.

"Those men are impossible," a colonel told him. Not so, Douglas thought. No group of men is impossible. For MacArthur, the assignment was difficult but exciting. He studied, encouraged his men, and worked hard. He stressed pride in soldiering. Soon the company led all the others. It became the best.

This sheet music cover shows the attitude of many people in the United States as the first troops were sent overseas to fight World War I. Most young men thought fighting the war would be a great adventure. They soon learned how terrible it was. Out of every 100 soldiers who fought, 63 were killed.

∾ THREE ∾

Leading
the Rainbow

*"To this day I feel a thrill whenever I see the
Rainbow's colorful patch."*
—Douglas MacArthur

Two shots from a pistol—and Archduke Francis
Ferdinand, heir to the throne of Austria-Hungary, and his
wife, Sophie, were dead. The assassin had jumped onto the
running board of their royal touring car. People from all over
the world, in all their different languages cried, "Murder!
Murder! How terrible!" The leaders of Austria-Hungary
believed the killer came from Serbia. On July 28, 1914, they
declared war on Serbia, the small country that is known today
as Yugoslavia. World War I had begun.

By October 30, Austria-Hungary, Germany, and the
Ottoman Empire (Turkey) were at war with Belgium, France,
Great Britain, Russia, and Serbia.

America was not yet involved, but military leaders in the
United States began to plan for war. The National Defense Act
of 1916 provided for the establishment of a 400,000-man

National Guard. Although Congress declared war on Germany on April 6, 1917, the Selective Service Act, which allowed men to be drafted into the regular army, was not passed until May 18. People in the War Department disagreed about whether or not the National Guard should help fight in the war. MacArthur believed in these citizen-soldiers and Secretary of War Newton Baker agreed with him. He sent for MacArthur.

"Get your cap," Baker said. "We are going to the White House."

For more than an hour, Baker and MacArthur argued in favor of using the National Guard. Finally President Wilson agreed. His decision was taken to Brigadier General William Mann. MacArthur told Mann, "We should form a division of units using the Guard from several states." General Mann agreed and said troops might be drawn from as many as 26 states. MacArthur said, "Fine, that will stretch over the whole country like a rainbow." That is how the 42nd Division became known as the Rainbow Division.

Soon after his discussion with General Mann, MacArthur visited with Secretary Baker. MacArthur told him that the best colonel on the general staff should be appointed chief.

"I have already made my selection for that post," the secretary said. "It is you."

"But I'm only a major," MacArthur replied.

Baker put his arm on MacArthur's shoulders. "You're wrong. You've just skipped two grades. You are now a colonel."

Then MacArthur surprised Baker. "I will not go with the engineers," he said. "From now on, I'm infantry."

∽

The 42nd Division assembled on Long Island, New York. It included infantrymen, artillerymen, engineers, machine gunners, military police, munitions experts, ambulance drivers, and cavalrymen. General Mann was the commander, MacArthur was the chief of staff. For two months they worked day and night to prepare 27,000 men for battle. No leaves were granted, and very few passes were given. Officers and enlisted men were treated alike.

On October 18, 1917, soldiers of the Rainbow Division were ready to leave for France. They fell in line and boarded a train that rocked and tooted toward the Brooklyn waterfront. There, ferryboats waited to take them across the bay to troopships on the New Jersey side.

Patriotic women from the town of Hoboken, New Jersey, greeted the soldiers and served them apple pie. Whistles blew, flags waved. People cried and hugged each other. Then the men walked up the gangplank of the *Covington,* a big ship that was part of a large convoy. They waved good-bye and started their journey across the Atlantic Ocean.

The trip was difficult. The men were drilled, drilled, drilled. Lifebelts were worn all the time. The ship was crowded and at night it was kept completely dark.

As night fell, MacArthur stood on the bridge, chewed on his corncob pipe, and stared at the black sea. "Why do you look out there?" an officer who was a new acquaintance asked.

"I'm wondering where my brother is," Douglas MacArthur said. Captain Arthur MacArthur was commanding one of the ships that came to protect the troops.

"I thought you might be worried about German subs."

"That, too," MacArthur said.

The *Covington* zigzagged through the ocean for 13 days. Then, 40 miles from port, it ran aground. At the same time, an enemy submarine was spotted. Seven patrol boats came to protect the transport, while the rest of the convoy sailed into port.

Scenes like the one above *took place all over the country as family members and friends said good-bye to the boys headed off to war.* Below, *soldiers fight in the trenches in France.*

When the *Covington* was set free, no berths (places where ships lie when at a dock) were left at the docks, so it lay anchored for three days. While he waited to go ashore, MacArthur stood on deck and looked at France through a drizzling rain. "I wonder," he said. "I wonder what the war will bring."

∾

Finally, the Rainbow Division set foot on French soil. French officers were assigned to work under MacArthur's command. "Our methods will be our own," he told his men, "but the French have had experience in trench warfare so we will listen to the advice they have to give us."

After a month of training, the Rainbow Division received orders to go farther into France. Because there were no trains or trucks to carry the troops, the day after Christmas the soldiers departed on foot. The doughboys (infantry soldiers) marched for three days from Rimaucourt to Rolampont. They shivered from the cold. They wiped snow from their faces. Some were without coats; others were without underwear or shoes. Although the division had been well equipped at Camp Mills, where they trained, much of their clothing and supplies had been taken over by G.H.Q. (general headquarters) to supply other divisions. By the last day, feet were bleeding and blotches of blood were left behind on the snow. It was a real test for the division, but from this march the spirit of the Rainbow was born.

At Rolampont, the troops settled in tents, and MacArthur concentrated on his paperwork. He delegated more authority to majors and lieutenant colonels. He worked early in the morning making notes and drawing maps. There was a plan behind his behavior: he wanted his staff to be self-sufficient so he could cross no-man's-land with his troops. No-man's-land.

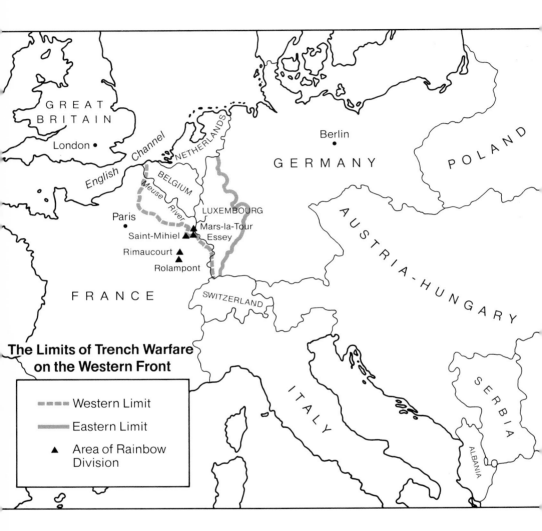

The Limits of Trench Warfare on the Western Front

- - - - Western Limit
———— Eastern Limit
▲ Area of Rainbow Division

That's what the troops called the battlefields between the two front lines. It was a place where no person should be.

One night the French planned a raid against the German lines. MacArthur asked General Georges de Bazelaire for permission to accompany the troops into battle.

The general was shocked. "It is unheard of for a commanding officer to take such a risk."

MacArthur argued, "I cannot fight them if I cannot see them."

The general wanted to refuse the request, but he soon gave in to MacArthur.

This was one of the times when MacArthur displayed his unusual personality. Instead of wearing a steel helmet, he pulled on his smashed-down hat. He wore a turtleneck sweater and riding breeches instead of an army uniform. Around his neck hung a four-foot muffler that his mother had knitted. A cigarette holder dangled from his lips, and a riding crop was his only weapon. When a soldier commented on his strange, non-regulation costume, MacArthur said, "It's the orders you disobey that make you famous." MacArthur sometimes used poor judgment. The truth is, he would have had less trouble in his army career if he had followed the rules as he had done at West Point.

Nevertheless, dressed in his costume, MacArthur rubbed sticky black mud on his face as the French soldiers did. He stuck wire cutters and a trench knife in his pocket, then checked with the fighting troops to see if they were ready.

"Let's go."

"Okay. Over the top."

Cutting through a tangled barbed wire fence, MacArthur and a group of French soldiers crawled over a mound of earth and sneaked toward the enemy.

Slowly they went, sometimes crawling, sometimes dashing forward in the hush of the night. When they got close, a German guard heard them. An alarm spread through the trenches. Flares soared and machine guns rattled but the advancing troops leaped into ditches or holes, called dugouts. The fighting was savage until a grenade, tossed into a dugout where the surviving Germans had fled, finally ended it.

When the troops returned with their prisoners at daybreak, the French soldiers crowded around MacArthur. His actions had been unusual for a soldier of such high rank. They shook his hand and slapped him on the back. He received a Silver Star for his bravery and a journalist wrote that "Colonel MacArthur is one of the ablest officers in the United States Army and also one of the most popular."

～

War raged in Europe from June 28, 1914 until November 1918. It was a time of great terror for people in almost every part of the world. At the front, where the most savage fighting took place, a chain of snakelike trenches stretched between the English Channel and the Swiss border. Facing each other across no-man's-land, armies squatted in candlelit dugouts. Men lay on their stomachs in ditches lined with bags of sand. The stench of urine burned their nostrils. The sight and overpowering smell of feces and decaying flesh made them want to vomit. Bullets cracked. Shells sang. Mustard gas hovered near the ground. The life expectancy of a machine gunner in battle was 30 minutes. This was life at the front during World War I. The MacArthur legend grew because of the way he conducted himself in these surroundings. Doughboys called him "the fighting Dude." The Germans believed he had a charmed life.

When the Germans surrendered, bombs stopped exploding, gunfire ceased, armed aircraft flew back to their bases, and submarines sailed back to their ports. But human suffering and devastated property were left behind. Almost 10 million soldiers died as a result of the war and some historians believe

Brigadier General Douglas MacArthur being decorated with the distinguished Service Cross by General of the Armies John Pershing shortly after World War I in Germany. MacArthur, who had become a hero during the war, also received decorations from other countries.

that as many civilians died as soldiers. By 1918, the cost of the war was $10 million an hour.

In every country, people were saying, "Never again!"

After World War I, MacArthur was appointed superintendent of West Point. With his mother, he lived in the house above.

MacArthur, right, *with his first wife, Louise Brooks MacArthur, in the Philippine Islands, in the early 1920s. Two of MacArthur's aides are to the left.*

❧ FOUR ❧

New Challenges

"DUTY, HONOR, COUNTRY"
—The motto of the Academy

MacArthur had become a hero during the war. He was awarded the American Distinguished Service Medal along with decorations from other countries. World War I had ended.

After the war, MacArthur and his troops were sent to Germany. They were to make sure the terms of the armistice, were being obeyed. The following April, they got orders to return home.

"It's time to leave," MacArthur told his men. "Our orders have come."

The soldiers walked up the gangplank and boarded the troopship *Leviathan*. Some of the men cried because of friends they were leaving behind. Others wiped tears of joy from their cheeks because they were going home. The big ship blew its whistle, pulled away from the dock, and headed out across the Atlantic.

MacArthur occupied a suite that had four rooms and three baths. It would have cost an ordinary traveler $5,000. His sheets were changed every day and he bathed every evening. Lower-ranking officers and enlisted men did not occupy such fine staterooms, but they were so happy to be out of the trenches that they did not complain.

During daylight hours, soldiers leaned on the rail and watched other ships in their convoy. They watched water curl and foam along the sides of the *Leviathan*. They watched the sun come up in the morning and sink into the sea at night. Then one day they watched buildings appear on the horizon. The troopship was coming into New York harbor. "There she is!" a soldier shouted. He was talking about the Statue of Liberty. The soldiers' hearts pounded with a new excitement, but they were soon disappointed. They had thought the pier would be crowded with people to welcome them. They had expected to be greeted as heroes. But, when their ship docked, the pier was vacant. No crowds were waiting. No bands were playing. No flags were waving.

"Who are you?" a little boy asked when they walked down the gangplank.

"We're soldiers from the famous 42nd," a sergeant replied.

The little boy wrinkled his brow and shook his head, "The 42nd?"

"That's right," the soldier said, thinking that the child might have heard of it.

It was no use. Feeling sad and lonely, the soldiers turned to each other. They shook hands, hugged, and said good-bye. It was the end of the Rainbow.

〰

For MacArthur, new adventures lay ahead. On June 12, 1919, he returned to West Point as its superintendent. Pinky was happy to be with her son. The two of them moved into the superintendent's mansion.

The academy had changed during the war. It had become easier for students to enter because its scholastic standards were lower. Pride in the institution had been lost, however, and MacArthur did not like what he saw. He wanted the honor of West Point to be restored. He was determined to make it happen, but bringing about change was difficult. Americans did not want to think about the chance of another war and they did not want to spend money educating military officers. "War is terrible; we must never fight again," was heard all over the country. The people wanted peace.

Though MacArthur also hated the pain and suffering that war brought, he thought that nations would not always agree. There would be boundaries to protect and ideals that could not be sacrificed. "So," he said, "America must be strong and able to defend its borders. Freedom is worth fighting for and must never be lost."

During the war, West Point had become a one-year school. Before long, standards of scholarship were renewed and it again became a four-year institutuon. Cadets were expected to be physically fit and able to work in teams. Warlike maneuvers were introduced, and brutal hazing disappeared. Athletics were important and they included soccer, track, basketball, golf, tennis, baseball, and football. The Point became a better school, but because there was not enough money, and because people did not wish to think about another war, MacArthur was disappointed that he was not able to accomplish more.

∽

Whether at war or peacefully at home, some form of excitement always seemed to be present in MacArthur's life.

In the front row, from left to right, *are MacArthur, Manuel Quezon, Sergio Osmena, and Manuel Roxas. Major General Douglas MacArthur was assigned to the Philippine Islands between 1922 and 1928. Quezon, Osmena, and Roxas were all future presidents of the Philippines.*

For example, one pitch-black night when his chauffeur was driving him home, a man with a flashlight jumped out of the bushes and stood in front of his car.

"Stop," MacArthur shouted.

His chauffeur slammed on the brakes and the car skidded to a halt.

"It's a holdup," the gunman said. He raised his pistol and demanded MacArthur's wallet.

"You don't get it as easily as that," the General called to him. "I've got around 40 dollars, but you'll have to whip me to get it. I'm getting out of this car, and I'll fight you for it."

The thug took a step forward. "I'll kill you," he said.

"Sure, you can shoot me," MacArthur told him. "But if

you do, they'll run you down, and you'll fry in the big house. Put down that gun and I'll come out and fight you fair and square for my money." Stepping into the street, the General said, "My name is MacArthur, and I live—"

"My God," the man gasped, "why didn't you tell me in the first place? Why, I was in the Rainbow. . . . My God, General, I'm sorry. I apologize."

∽

During his tour of duty at West Point, MacArthur married Mrs. Louise Brooks, a wealthy divorcée with two small children, Walter and Louise. Pinky was very angry with her son's choice. She moved out of the mansion and refused to attend the wedding.

When his tour ended at the academy, MacArthur and his new family sailed to the Philippines. On October 22, 1922, their transport ship docked at Pier Five in Manila. Once again, the General looked across the bay at the cliffs of Bataan and the island of Corregidor. Eighteen years had passed, and many changes had taken place. Roads had been improved in the city and new buildings stood along them.

Though he loved the islands and their people, these years were not happy ones for MacArthur. His brother died, his assignments were difficult, and his marriage was not succeeding.

MacArthur became known as "General MacArthur the Younger." Like "General MacArthur the Elder," he worked well with the Asian people. He was dedicated to his duty, even when he was asked to carry out a task usually performed by a lower-ranking officer. He had been ordered to survey the mountains of Bataan.

"Why that's a job for a young engineer officer, not a job for a brigadier general," said George Cochu, who had once been MacArthur's roommate at the Point and was now a major on his staff.

"I know you are right," MacArthur said, "but this time I will obey orders."

He mapped 40 square miles of land that was infested with mosquitos that carried malaria. He trudged up mountains that were high and steep. He pushed through thickets of bamboo.

"Why?" Cochu asked again.

"Because Pershing ordered it."

"Why would General Pershing do such a thing?"

"I believe he is angry with me," MacArthur told him.

General Pershing had been in love with Louise Brooks. The story goes that Pershing was upset when Louise left him to go with MacArthur. This may have been more rumor than truth. In any case, MacArthur did his work well, and Pershing promoted him to major general on January 17, 1925. Since his new rank made him overqualified for his work in the Philippines, he was transferred to Baltimore.

The move came just in time, because Louise was becoming more and more unhappy in Manila. The weather had been hot and uncomfortable. There had been no parties to attend. Young Walter had been injured when he fell off a horse, and little Louise had become ill with malaria.

∽

Soon after he arrived in Baltimore, MacArthur was appointed head of the United States Olympic Committee. Because of MacArthur's energy and flair for the unusual, U.S. participation in the 1928 games became a MacArthur production. A reporter from the *Paris Tribune* recalled that the general was forceful, articulate, thoughtful, and well read. There is no doubt that he dominated the U.S. contingent.

As head of the U.S. Olympic Committee, MacArthur marched in the opening day parade of the 19th Olympiad in Amsterdam, Holland. Third in line, Major General MacArthur salutes the crowd as he passes. John Weissmuller is the standard bearer, and C. L. Houser is the flag bearer.

And he had not lost his determination to come in first at whatever he did. When the manager of the U.S. boxing team threatened to withdraw, MacArthur set his jaw and growled, "Americans never quit." Striding back and forth before his athletes, he said: "We are here to represent the greatest country on earth. We did not come here to lose gracefully. We came to win. . . ." And win they did.

Shortly after MacArthur finished his Olympic report to President Coolidge, he was ordered to return to Manila and assume command of all forces in the Philippines.

"No assignment could have pleased me more," he said. Nothing could have pleased his wife less. He returned to the islands alone, and his wife filed for divorce.

General Douglas MacArthur when he served as chief of staff of the United States Army

✑ FIVE ✑

Reaching the Top

"If only your father could see you now!
Douglas, you're everything he wanted to be."
—Mrs. Arthur (Pinky) MacArthur

On August 6, 1930, President Hoover announced MacArthur's appointment as army chief of staff. The assignment did not make him happy because he wanted to stay with his troops in the Philippines. He was going to refuse the promotion when his mother sent a cable and asked him to accept. The cable read: "Your father would be ashamed of you if you refuse the position." That settled it. He sailed home on September 19. On November 21 he pinned the fourth star on his uniform. He was the eighth American to earn the position of four-star general.

MacArthur had been in military service for 31 years. During that time he had received orders and obeyed them as best he could. Now his position was changed. He would not only be giving and taking orders, he would also have to determine policy and make many important decisions.

MacArthur and his mother moved into a brick mansion on the banks of the Potomac River. Even though it was the number one quarters at Fort Myer, MacArthur felt it needed improvements. He ordered the installation of an elevator and a sun porch for his mother.

Pinky was happy. Her son was successful, and she was with him. One day she fingered the stars on her son's uniform and whispered, "If only your father could see you now! Douglas, you're everything he wanted to be."

During his first few months as chief of staff, MacArthur kept a low profile. He did not attend parties. He granted few interviews and his name seldom appeared in newspaper gossip columns.

But he could not keep his unusual personality a secret. It soon became known that he sat at his desk wearing a Japanese kimono while he cooled himself with an Oriental fan. It was whispered that the new chief of staff smoked cigarettes held in a jeweled holder, and spoke of himself in the third person. ("MacArthur will be leaving now.") He had a 15-foot mirror hung behind his office chair so that his reflection could be seen. These things earned him the reputation of being a show-off.

During part of 1932, MacArthur traveled through Europe inspecting military bases. On these trips he rode by himself in a private railroad car. How important he must have felt as the train rumbled across the continent from country to country. In France he was presented with the Grand Cross of the Legion of Honor. King Alexander greeted him in Yugoslavia. Heads of government welcomed him in Rumania, Hungary, Poland, and Austria.

But there were unhappy times for MacArthur, too. One of the most painful episodes during his role as chief of staff was

One of MacArthur's duties as chief of staff was to inspect European military bases. He traveled through many countries. Above, he poses with Polish military leaders.

the Bonus March, which took place in 1932, the third year of the Great Depression. Millions of people were out of work. Their families were hurting. Late in May, an army of hungry veterans arrived in Washington, D.C. They were hoping to get early payment on a bonus that had been promised to them for their wartime service. Originally, the bonus was not due until 1945, but in 1931 Congress provided payment for half of the bonus. During the summer of 1932, Congress was considering payment of the other half. For two months the veterans lived in old buildings along Pennsylvania Avenue. They made daily marches to the Capitol to try to convince Congress to pass the legislation. Members of Congress did not listen to their pleas. No one seemed to care about their needs. Senator J. Hamilton Louis said, "Veterans are causing fellow countrymen to wonder whether their soldiers served for patriotism or merely for pay." The days dragged on. The men grew tired and dirty. Their clothes were wearing out. They needed money for themselves and for their families back home. Tensions grew. Nerves were on edge.

Seventeen thousand men spread their bedrolls in vacant lots. At night they squatted by burning campfires. The governor of New York, Franklin D. Roosevelt, offered New Yorkers railroad fares if they would leave Washington. President Hoover put a bill through Congress authorizing loans for transportation. With money for travel, most of the veterans picked up their belongings and returned to their homes. MacArthur thought most of the men who stayed had not fought in the war. He thought they were thugs out to cause trouble.

Many people became angry with the General. But MacArthur would not back down. He believed that Communist leaders had seized the opportunity to make America look bad. According to MacArthur, they started battles in the streets and threw stones at the Washington police. Men who held important offices were threatened. The crowd was out of control.

"Bring law and order," Hoover told his chief of staff.

MacArthur thought the president was acting just in time. He took 600 soldiers with him to carry out the task. Among the men were Major Dwight D. Eisenhower (Ike) and Major George S. Patton. The president thought the sight of federal troops would be enough to make the marchers leave, but he was wrong. The men fought back. A veteran yelled at MacArthur, "You crummy old bum!" Another shouted, "The American flag means nothing to me after this." Then real trouble developed.

Hoover had ordered MacArthur to leave the marchers' tents and lean-tos alone. Instead of following orders, he rode into their makeshift village and had their shanties torched.

The Bonus March of 1932 caused many people to become angry with MacArthur. In defiance of presidential orders, the shanties of the marchers were torched, and a seven-year-old boy was bayoneted.

People from all over the United States were angry and strongly denounced MacArthur for his part in the raid. He was pictured, in full-dress uniform, riding on a fiery white charger and waving a bloody saber. But he did not believe what he had done was wrong. He was proud that no shots had been fired even though the rioters had attacked the soldiers with sticks, stones, and clubs. MacArthur claimed that no one had been killed and that there had been no serious injuries. But other reports noted that two babies had died of tear gas and a seven-year-old boy had been bayoneted through the leg while trying to rescue his pet rabbit.

In 1933, Franklin Delano Roosevelt succeeded Hoover as president. The country's economy was still depressed. Men and women needed jobs. Families needed money for house payments, food, and clothing.

President Franklin Delano Roosevelt, above left, *created the Civilian Conservation Corps,* above right and below, *which provided training and employment for two million young men.*

"We must do something for our unemployed," the new president said.

The Civilian Conservation Corps was created to help the unemployed, and MacArthur was put in charge. The Corps provided training and employment for two million young men. They cleared ground and made parks. They built dams, made trails through wooded acres, and fought forest fires.

MacArthur worked hard to make the Corps a success, but he was constantly reminded that the army was undersupplied and understaffed. He sincerely believed that the greatest democracy in the world should be the strongest militarily. He did not believe peace would come from weakness. But he stood alone in his beliefs, or so it seemed.

In every state of the union, there were people who thought that war could never come again. Many members of Congress were annoyed with military leaders who disagreed with this view. MacArthur, however, wanted to inform the citizens of the United States of the need to be prepared. In a speech he gave at the University of Pittsburgh he said, "History has proved that nations once great, that neglected their national defense are now dust and ashes...." He was trying to tell people that if countries are not willing to protect themselves, they might be taken over by those which are stronger.

The people's reaction was quick. "We don't want to hear about war," was shouted from every corner of America. MacArthur was criticized in newspapers and on the radio. His warnings were ignored.

❧

Dwight D. Eisenhower became MacArthur's assistant in 1935. Many years later when a woman asked Ike if he knew MacArthur he said, "Not only have I met him, ma'am; I studied dramatics under him for five years in Washington and four years in the Philippines." But Eisenhower also wrote: "The General was a rewarding man to work for," one who never cared what hours were kept and, once he had given an assignment, never asked any questions. "His only requirement was that the work be done."

Ike soon discovered that his superior officer was well read and could converse on almost any subject. He also learned that MacArthur did not discuss, he told. Monologues were his specialty. The General's wealth of information came from his unusual memory. When he read through a typewritten page once, he could repeat almost all of it word for word.

∞

In 1934 MacArthur had completed his four-year term as chief of staff, but President Roosevelt decided to keep him in that post for one more year. The president also decided MacArthur's next move. "Douglas," he said, "I want you to go to the Philippines as a military adviser."

MacArthur's good-byes in Washington were pleasant. He was awarded another Distinguished Service Medal. The president told him, "Douglas, if war should suddenly come, don't wait for orders to come home. Grab the first transportation you can find. I want you to command my armies."

The *Washington Herald* printed, "Brilliant and magnetic General Douglas MacArthur is going out as chief of staff in a blaze of splendid glory."

∞ SIX ∞

Defending
the Philippines

"Keep your faith in America, whatever happens."
—Manuel Quezon

Eisenhower was with MacArthur on a westbound train to San Francisco when the General received a telegram announcing that Major General Malin Craig would take his place as chief of staff. From San Francisco, MacArthur would travel by boat to the Philippines.

MacArthur was happy with the assignment because he wanted the Filipinos to build a strong army. He wanted them to be able to defend themselves. He felt he could help.

But he did have one problem. His mother was ill and he did not wish to leave her. When Pinky realized that her son might refuse this fine position, she offered to go with him.

Three majors traveled with MacArthur, one of them an army physician who attended Pinky. Together they boarded the *President Hoover* in San Francisco. While they were sailing across the Pacific, MacArthur met Jean Faircloth. They became friends and before long he was inviting her to breakfast. They ate, visited, and walked the decks together. But most important of all, Jean decided to extend her trip, originally to Shanghai, and sail with him to Manila.

It was autumn when MacArthur returned for the fifth time to the city he loved. "This time is for keeps," he said as he looked about at Manila's high walls and churches.

MacArthur and his small party moved into a white concrete, red-roofed hotel on Dewey Boulevard. The MacArthurs occupied the six-room, air-conditioned penthouse. The General was happy to have his mother with him, but her health became increasingly worse. They had been in Manila only two months when Pinky slipped into a deep sleep and died.

∽

MacArthur had settled the Eisenhowers in the hotel's new wing, and now he began adjusting to living alone. He was now 60 years old but looked 20 years younger. He walked tall in his immaculate military uniform and was someone whom the Filipino people looked upon with awe. They loved their new leader and before long they gave him a rank that no other American soldier has ever had. Manuel Quezon, their president, made him a field marshal.

MacArthur was surprised and flattered. He wanted to look very grand for the ceremony so he designed a fancy costume: black pants and a white top covered with medals, stars, and gold cord. With it he wore a braided cap, which later became famous in World War II. For this occasion he was truly a show-off, but he dressed for the Filipinos, who liked his style. On August 24, 1936, Aurora Quezon, the first lady of the Philippines, presented him with a gold baton. He had become the highest paid soldier in the world.

More and more often he now arrived at social functions with Miss Faircloth. Later MacArthur said, "She was my constant companion."

During this time, rumblings of war could be heard in Europe and Asia. MacArthur was short of supplies for his army. Soldiers were issued helmets that were soft and tennis shoes that wore out during their first maneuvers. These were not the only mistakes the Americans made. They misjudged the Japanese people. American soldiers thought the Japanese were a comical race. They wrote backward. They built their houses from the roof down. They pulled their saws instead of pushing them. Department store "bargain b sements" were on the top floor. When American soldiers saw Japan's aircraft flying overhead, they were quick to say, "Those ships can't be flown by Japanese. They can't be such good pilots."

In his office, MacArthur pushed his hands into his pockets and paced back and forth. He paused behind his desk, flipped open a small box, and took out a slim cigar. He thought aloud. "Japan's armies have gone into Manchuria. They're overrunning China. American planes have spotted troopships heading south." That was during the summer of 1937.

During those worrisome months for MacArthur, Jean had continued to be the General's best friend. They had been married during a quick trip to New York on April 30, 1937. On February 21, 1938, she gave birth to their son. They named him Arthur, and he became the delight of his father's life.

One year later, Adolf Hitler's German aircraft flew over Poland and bombed its cities. Poland surrendered, and the German armies marched across the borders of six more

Douglas and Jean Faircloth MacArthur on their wedding day in New York on April 30, 1937. They met on board the President Hoover *while sailing to the Philippines.*

countries. The people of Denmark, Norway, Belgium, Luxembourg, the Netherlands, and France lost their freedom.

War had broken out in Europe, just as MacArthur had predicted. MacArthur felt that the United States would soon be part of it and he feared that the war would spread to Asia. His heart pounded. He felt that now it was very important to have one leader for the armies in the Far East.

In 1941 MacArthur cabled Washington suggesting that he be made commander of all soldiers in the Philippine archipelago (islands). This meant that both armies, United States and Filipino, would have one leader. "We need to be stronger," he said over and over again. "We need to hurry."

Return cables told him to be patient and wait.

At the same time, President Roosevelt gave orders which angered the Japanese people. Anything in the United States that was owned by Japan could not be moved or sold. The Panama Canal was closed to Japanese shipping. Americans were told they could not send oil, iron, or rubber to Japan.

On July 27, when the General sat down to breakfast with his newspaper, he glanced at words that were outlined on the corner of the front page. They said that President Roosevelt was mobilizing the island's forces and that MacArthur would lead them. "Just what I wanted," MacArthur said. "A Far East army with one commander." When a cable came confirming the news, MacArthur sent for his aides. "I feel like an old dog in a new uniform," he said.

A friend warned him, "The task will be difficult, almost too much for one man."

MacArthur paced the room. He walked to the window and looked out across Manila Bay. "These islands must and will be defended," he said. "I can but do my best."

Japan had six million men in uniform, but the American

people had been slow to see the danger of war. MacArthur needed supplies. Back in the United States, factories started to work three shifts daily, but they weren't producing enough. Even after crates were filled and delivered to piers, a six-week voyage to Manila lay ahead. And then . . .

～

At 7:55 A.M. on December 7, 1941, Japanese aircraft attacked United States military bases in the Hawaiian Islands. About 360 planes swooped down on the Pacific fleet and army aircraft at Hickam Field. This surprise attack killed 3,700 American servicemen. Eight battleships were lost, three light cruisers, three destroyers, four other vessels, and about 170 planes.

General MacArthur lifted the telephone on his night table to hear the news. "Pearl Harbor!" he repeated into the mouthpiece as if he could not believe what he was hearing. "Pearl Harbor! It should be our strongest point!"

At 3:40 A.M. MacArthur dressed while his officers and Quezon gathered. The General looked gray, ill, and exhausted. MacArthur was in shock. He could not think. He could not plan. He could not make decisions. Like a machine that was overloaded, his mind was stuck.

When daylight broke, all of Manila was in a state of confusion. Warships bobbed up and down in the bay; troops lacked instructions; most of the pilots were recovering from a party; and Clark Field did not have a single air raid shelter. Officers wondered what to do. Six hours after the attack on Pearl Harbor, MacArthur was still delaying action. But Quezon had already given a handwritten statement to a reporter. It said: "The zero hour has arrived. I expect every Filipino—man and woman—to do his duty. We have pledged our honor to stand by the United States and we shall not

Japanese aircraft conducted a successful surprise attack on Pearl Harbor on December 7, 1941. Many ships and planes were destroyed, and 3700 servicemen were killed.

fail her. . . ." These words could be heard again and again over every radio in the Philippine Islands.

Shortly before noon, a radar operator picked up blips of approaching aircraft. Its V formation was pointing toward Clark Field. There were 200 of them flying at 25,000 feet. Warnings were sent to Clark by teletype, by radio, and by telephone. The messages did not get through by teletype because the pilots, who should have received them, were at lunch. Static kept other messages from being understood.

The planes swooped down and dropped their bombs. Fuel tanks exploded. Buildings burst into flame and all aircraft were destroyed. Jean MacArthur and three-year-old Arthur

Manuel Quezon, president of the Commonwealth of the Philippines, left, *and Douglas MacArthur,* right, *on the day MacArthur was appointed commander of the Far East forces.*

stood in their apartment and watched columns of oily black smoke rise over Manila. As far away as Washington there were angry cries, "What happened? Was the army asleep?"

Four days after the attack on Hawaii, Germany and Italy declared war on the United States. The Japanese had landed on Luzon and were advancing south. Schools were closed in Manila, and women and children moved to the country. Men stayed behind to dig shelters, build sandbag walls, and fill garbage cans with water for drinking.

Finally, General MacArthur began to act like himself. Alert now, he realized that if he did not move he would be caught between two arms of the Japanese army. "Bataan," he said as he studied his map. "We must go to Bataan." General Pershing called the decision "one of the greatest moves in all military history."

Troops and equipment headed for Bataan while three divisions and a cavalry regiment held the Japanese army. The only way to reach Bataan was over land, then across the Calumpit Bridge which spanned the rushing Pampanga River. When they reached the other side of the river, they planned to blow up the bridge.

Naval guns and Long Toms (cannons) crossed first. Then for two days and two nights, there was a 10-mile-long traffic jam of taxis, trucks, buses, horse-drawn carriages, limousines, oxcarts, and anything else that could carry refugees. Finally, early in the morning on December 31, the Philippine army followed. The last infantryman passed over at 5:00 A.M. MacArthur now had 80,000 fighting men and 26,000 refugees on Bataan.

Destroying the bridge was postponed while the army waited for stragglers. When dawn broke, Japanese could be seen moving through the jungle. "Blow it!" called the officer in charge. "Blow the bridge!"

General MacArthur had saved the army and many civilians. Now his problem was feeding them.

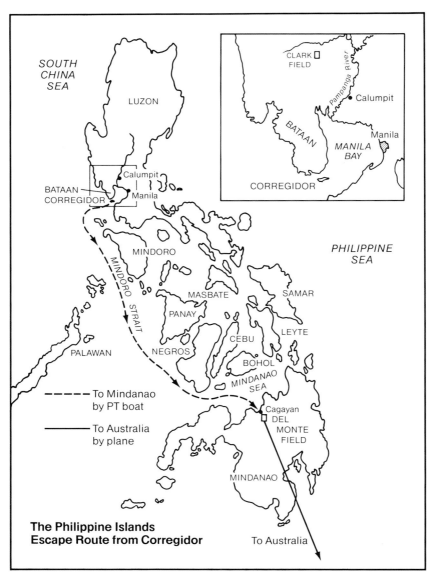

The Philippine Islands
Escape Route from Corregidor

*Early in 1943, MacArthur was ordered to leave the Philippines
and proceed to Australia. This map shows the route he used to
escape from Corregidor to Mindanao by PT boat, and then from
Del Monte Field on Mindanao to Australia by plane.*

∽ SEVEN ∽

Days of Anguish

"They are leaving us one by one."
—Carlos Romulo

To protect Manila from ground and air attacks by the Japanese, MacArthur decided to evacuate (withdraw) all military forces and declare Manila an open city. By international law, an open city is not defended or occupied by military forces. Because the city has no defenses, enemy forces are not supposed to bombard it.

"We're leaving," he told Jean. "You have four hours to pack. And tell Ah Cheu that she's going with us." Ah Cheu was Arthur's nanny and the MacArthurs thought of her as part of their family.

MacArthur had decided to put his headquarters on Corregidor, a small island off the Bataan peninsula. Corregidor was only 30 miles across the bay from Manila, but the steamer they were taking was small. The captain said that everyone could take only one suitcase.

"One suitcase," Jean muttered as she packed. "Only one suitcase." She tried to collect her thoughts while bombs rocked nearby buildings. Quickly she reached for her brown coat. She jerked dresses off their hangers, grabbed a pair of shoes, and tossed in a tiny box of jewelry along with a few toilet articles. The rest of the space was taken by food and clothes for Arthur. Jean looked at the small pile of belongings and wondered how many weeks—maybe months—she would have to make do with only those few things that lay folded in the suitcase.

One hundred people gathered on the dock. It was Christmas Eve, 1942, and the travelers were sad to be leaving decorated trees and packages that had been quickly opened and set aside.

It was a moon-bright night. The small party climbed aboard a little ship that rocked up and down and squeaked against the dock. Across the bay, smoke drifted from oil fields that had been bombed by the enemy. As the passengers cast one last look toward Manila, the ship's engines roared. MacArthur, his family, and his staff were off into the night. No one spoke. It was so crowded, the General could not pace.

❧

Corregidor, called "the Rock," is shaped like a pollywog, or tadpole. It has three rising terraces. On the very top of the Rock stood a little white church which flew a United States flag. MacArthur's main quarters, a 1,400-foot-long tunnel, held maps, desks, and radio equipment. Other passages housed hospital wards, storerooms, and ammunition.

The MacArthurs settled into a small gray cottage a quarter of a mile outside the tunnel's entrance. It was dangerous to be so high on the Rock where they could easily be seen by enemy aircraft, but Jean did not want to be away from her

Malinta Tunnel on Corregidor held MacArthur's main headquarters. Other passages were used for hospital wards, storerooms, and ammunition. Here and on Bataan peninsula, U.S. and Philippine forces made their last stand against the Japanese invaders.

husband. To protect her son she kept a car parked near the cottage. When the siren warned them that Japanese planes were coming, Jean, Arthur, and Ah Cheu ran to the car where a driver was waiting. "Here we go again," he'd shout as he sped them to the tunnel and safety.

Two days after their arrival, the Japanese knew where the General and his party were. At eight o'clock the following morning, 18 white, twin-engined airplanes appeared in the sky. They were headed straight for Corregidor.

Everyone but MacArthur ran for cover. He stood outside to watch the action. Between bombings, Jean would ask a soldier to find out what was happening to the General. The soldier would run outside and take a quick look. "The General is standing by a hedge," he'd say. "He has a cane under his arm. His cap is pushed back, and he's smoking."

∽

Living conditions on Bataan peninsula were almost impossible. Pythons wiggled through thick underbrush. It rained day and night. Drinking water was contaminated. Food was so scarce it was rationed, and soldiers and refugees were starving. As their hunger grew, they ate horses, monkeys, and deer. Roots, leaves, wild chickens, and pigs became part of their diet. The men became ill. Dirty clothes hung on their weakened bodies.

MacArthur sent messages to Roosevelt. "Our soldiers need food."

Roosevelt replied, "Food is coming."

Seventy-seven days after MacArthur set up his headquarters on Corregidor, a soldier left the peninsula and went to the Rock. "You must come," he said to MacArthur. "You must cheer up the men on Bataan."

MacArthur took the soldier's advice. What he saw made him sick. Although MacArthur had lost 25 pounds from lack of food, his men were actually starving. "Food is coming," he told them. "Roosevelt has promised. Food is coming." But all the food for the armies was being sent to the fighting men in Europe. It never reached the soldiers who were dying on Bataan.

MacArthur never went back to Bataan. Perhaps he was ashamed that he had misled his troops. Whatever his reason, he stayed on Corregidor. Angry American soldiers nicknamed him "Dugout Doug."

While men were starving on Bataan, and the navy was taking a beating on the high seas, Tokyo Rose, a Japanese woman, was broadcasting to American soldiers. "General MacArthur will be hanged in Tokyo's Imperial Plaza. He will be captured in a month. Give up, you foolish Americans. Spare your lives."

Morale was already low among the soldiers, when, in the United States, an irresponsible news reporter spoke into his microphone and sent a message to the Japanese army, "I dare you to bomb Corregidor!" They did bomb it. The first soldiers to see enemy aircraft shouted, "Meatball!" or "Scrambled eggs!" Men raced for the shelter of the tunnel. All but one. The General stayed outside to watch the enemy aircraft circling and diving.

~

Finally the day came when Roosevelt no longer promised food. The Philippines had been written off. "There are times," the secretary of war said, "when men have to die." Then a message to MacArthur came over the radio at 11:23 A.M., February 23, Manila time, two months after MacArthur arrived on Corregidor. Decoded, the message ordered the General to proceed to Australia.

Once again MacArthur looked old, ill, and drained of confidence. His departure would be a blow to his heroic men. It would be a blow to civilians back home. He was going to resign from the army so he could stay on the Rock, but close friends and the president were able to change his mind. "You are needed," they said.

His most important good-bye was to General Wainwright. "If I get through to Australia you know I'll come back as soon as I can with as much as I can." He radioed that he would leave the Rock on March 15, and arrive in Australia on March 18. "We go with the fall of the moon," he said. Because of increased enemy naval activity, however, he was forced to set a new departure date—Wednesday, March 11, at sunset.

MacArthur knew that the Japanese had heard of his move. But to them, it probably seemed impossible for MacArthur to slip through 2,500 miles of enemy-controlled water.

MacArthur assembled his staff. He told them, "Buck (Lieutenant John D. Bulkeley) tells me we have a chance to get through the blockade in PT boats. It won't be easy. There will be plenty of risks. But four boats are available, and with machine guns and torpedoes we could put up a good fight. . . ."

That night the General radioed that he would need three B-17 airplanes to meet him at Mindanao's Del Monte Field. MacArthur issued more food-rationing orders for the troops on Bataan. He then drew up his passenger list. Besides his family and Arthur's nanny, the party included 13 army officers, two naval officers, and a staff sergeant.

Jean packed tins of salmon and canned orangeade. She took one dress, her coat, and a pantsuit. Ah Cheu carried her belongings in a handkerchief and Arthur clutched his stuffed rabbit, named Old Friend, and a toy motorcycle.

Evening was falling over Corregidor when four PT boats crept into the bay. The dock had been broken by bombs. Splintery boards crisscrossed the shore. Every building and tree had been burned. Bombs had dug enormous holes in the earth, and fires had left black streaks on rocks. Above the sloshing noise of the boats, two voices were heard.

"What's his chance of getting through?"

"Dunno. He's lucky. Maybe one in five."

At 9:15 P.M., four young skippers pushed their PTs' throttles forward. The boats crept through a minefield and out of the bay.

✑ EIGHT ✑

Reclaiming
the Philippines

"I shall return."
—Douglas MacArthur

The PT boats were squat and narrow. These boats, called "Green Dragons" by the Japanese, were designed to roar into battle, torpedo their targets, and get out in a hurry. But MacArthur's small fleet was old. Because the boats' engines were clogged with carbon and rust, they could not travel at full speed.

The bow of the boat slapped against the waves. Salt water sprayed over the passengers, soaking their clothes and stinging their faces. MacArthur, Arthur, and Ah Cheu were sick. The General wrote that it was "like a trip in a concrete mixer." But worse than the ride was the fear of being seen by the Japanese.

"Look," an officer shouted.

There was a bonfire on an island beach. Then another and another.

"They're signaling," someone cried. "They're telling Japanese ships we're out here."

Hearts pounded. Wet and afraid, the escapees slid down farther in the hull of the boat.

Thirty-five hours and 560 miles from the time they started, the exhausted crews pulled into safety at Mindanao. Feeling better now, the General stood on the prow of the boat, shook the salt water from his cap, and put the cap back on at a jaunty angle. It was March 13. They had made it through the dangerous waters, but their trip was not finished.

When he got on shore, the General paced. "I have to get to Melbourne," he said. "Where are my airplanes?"

Finally an old B-17 Flying Fortress arrived. The plane coughed and wheezed to a wobbly landing. MacArthur took one look at it and lost his temper. He would not board, or let any member of his crew board such a dangerous aircraft. Then he demanded "the three best planes in the United States or Hawaii," and, he said "they must be flown by experienced airmen."

New planes were sent, but they were still very rickety. Their pilots joked that the B-17s were tied together with chewing gum and baling wire.

"This is it," the captain said waving his hand toward the planes. "This is our best."

The Americans traveled at night, but Japanese "coast watchers" listened and watched the skies for aircraft. At sunrise Japanese fighters went in search of the B-17s. The American pilots knew they were being hunted. They maneuvered in, out, and through the clouds and once again they escaped. "It was close," MacArthur said when they landed in Australia, "but that's the way it is in war. You win or lose, live or die...." They were on the ground at Batchelor

Field but still only part of the way to Melbourne.

The crew ate breakfast in a little shack. Jean leaned on the table and said, "Never again will anybody get me into an airplane!"

MacArthur thought Jean was right. He decided they would travel the next part of their trip by car. Back in his room, friends and Major Morhouse, a medical officer, found MacArthur striding about in his underwear.

"What's the matter with you?" the doctor asked.

"They're just too lazy to do what I want," MacArthur raged. "I want a motorcade to the nearest train station."

The doctor shook his head, "You are wrong," he said. "Your son has been ill since leaving the Rock. I cannot be sure that he could make such a long drive across the desert." The nearest train station was a thousand miles away.

Quickly the General ordered DC-3s which took his party to Alice Springs and the railroad station. That evening on the train, Jean, a nurse, and Ah Cheu made up bunks, then they and Arthur crawled under the covers as the train clickety-clacked. The General stretched out on a bench and snored.

Across the Pacific Ocean and across the United States, President Roosevelt held a press conference in Washington, D.C. He told reporters that General MacArthur had escaped from Corregidor and was now "down under." (Australia is known as the Land Down Under because it is below the equator.)

On March 18, the *New York Times* headline read: MACARTHUR IN AUSTRALIA AS ALLIED COMMANDER.

In Germany he was described as the "fleeing general." In Rome Mussolini called him a "coward."

To the world, MacArthur said, "The President of the United States ordered me to break through the Japanese

When MacArthur arrived in Australia, he was given a hero's welcome. Above, *he is a guest of the Australian Parliament in Canberra, in March 1942.*

MacArthur's wife, Jean, sits with their son, Arthur, as he practices piano at their apartment in the Lennon Hotel in Brisbane, Australia, in December 1942.

lines . . . for the purpose . . . of organizing the American offensive against Japan. . . . I came through and I shall return."

"I shall return!" His words were shouted around the world, and they became a promise to the Filipino people. "I shall return" was drawn in the sands on beaches. It was written on walls and whispered in churches. Filipinos found the sentence in cartons of gum and matches left by American submarines. Some Japanese soldiers even found the sentence neatly written in a box of shells during battle.

∾

When the General's train finally pulled into Melbourne, 6,000 admirers were waiting. MacArthur and his small crew had made an 11-day, 3,000-mile trip from Corregidor. His greatest surprise of the war, however, was yet to come.

The army MacArthur thought was waiting for him did not exist. "Impossible!" the General stormed. "I've been tricked." He paced back and forth in his temporary headquarters. He was supreme commander of nothing.

∾

On April 25, a bedraggled soldier walked into MacArthur's office. Carlos Romulo had escaped from Bataan. He was unshaven. His ragged uniform hung loosely over his thin body. "Carlos, my boy!" MacArthur shouted. He cried and hugged him, saying, "I can't bear to look at you."

It was shortly after seeing Carlos that MacArthur heard of the Bataan Death March. The Japanese captured Corregidor on May 6 and marched their prisoners to Bataan. The next day, the 11,000 prisoners began the brutal Death March to the north. Between 7,000 and 10,000 died or were executed. Filled with sorrow for his men, he sent a message to his church in Little Rock, Arkansas. "I ask that you seek divine guidance for me in the great struggle that lies ahead."

After the Japanese captured Corregidor, they marched 11,000 starving prisoners north from Bataan. During the brutal march, thousands of prisoners died or were executed.

On April 18, 1943, a month after his arrival in Australia, President Roosevelt appointed MacArthur commander in chief of the Allied forces in the Southwest Pacific. MacArthur, who had been studying his maps, probably knew more about the geography of the Philippine Islands and the Pacific coastlines than any other man by then. "We'll attack," MacArthur said as he stood back and looked at his charts.

He pointed his corncob pipe toward the islands. "We'll hit 'em where they ain't . . . ," he said. "They won't expect us. Their small army will be easily beaten. Our losses will not be great."

"And then what will we do?" his aide asked.

"We'll build air bases, and move forward."

"And then...?"

"We won't fight where the Japanese are strong. We'll leap over the top of them and cut off their supplies. It will work," he said. "They'll starve." His plan became known as "leapfrogging."

MacArthur tapped his pipe in the ashtray. "We won't take the populated islands. I don't want them. Starvation and the jungle, they're my allies."

∽

MacArthur's Pacific force included men from several countries besides the United States. Men from Australia,

General of the Army Douglas MacArthur, commander in chief of the Allied forces in the Southwest Pacific

New Zealand, and the Philippine Islands were among them. Working together, the army, the navy, and the marines recaptured the Gilbert Islands, the Marshall Islands, New Guinea, Saipan, and other Japanese strongholds. One of the things they had to do was clear fields for aircraft. In 1943, during the New Guinea campaign, the General went with his men to Los Negros. While pulling their ship close to the shore, MacArthur's forces were attacked by the enemy's big guns. Bullets flew while MacArthur stood on the bow of the ship *Phoenix* and leaned on the rail.

"General," his men said, "you're in danger."

MacArthur lit his corncob pipe and waved out a match. "I want to get a sense of the situation," he said. Finally, blasts from the ship's guns wiped out the Japanese cannons and sent the enemy hurrying into the jungle. MacArthur left the ship to stroll ashore. As he walked from the beach and entered the forest, a lieutenant touched him on the sleeve. "Excuse me, sir," he said. "It isn't safe for you to walk here. We killed a Japanese sniper just a few minutes ago."

"Fine," the General said, stepping over dead Japanese, "that's what you should do."

∞

Back home in the United States, hard-working men and women had kept factories open around the clock. They were busy building ships, airplanes, and all other kinds of equipment needed by the armed forces fighting in Europe and the Pacific. Part of the results of their labor would soon be seen.

After almost two years of leapfrogging from island to island, fighting, digging in, and building airstrips, the day finally came when MacArthur could keep his promise and return to the Philippines. It was Friday, October 20, 1944—"A-Day."

In the U.S., people in factories worked around the clock to supply the armed forces. For the first time, many women were hired as factory workers.

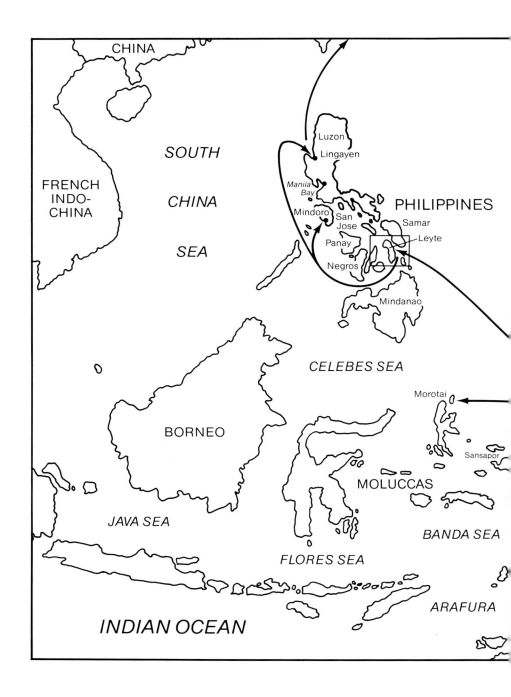

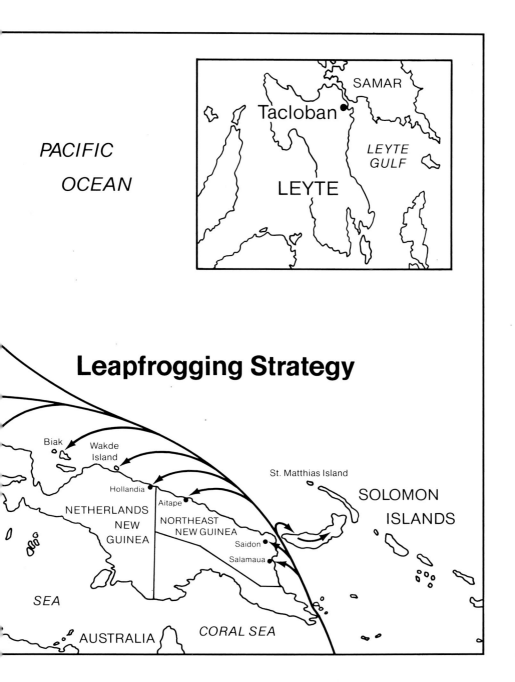

PACIFIC

OCEAN

SAMAR

Tacloban

LEYTE
GULF

LEYTE

Leapfrogging Strategy

Biak

Wakde
Island

St. Matthias Island

SOLOMON

ISLANDS

Hollandia

Aitape

NETHERLANDS
NEW
GUINEA

NORTHEAST
NEW GUINEA

Saidon

Salamaua

SEA

AUSTRALIA

CORAL SEA

"A-Day!" MacArthur paced the deck of the ship, the *Nashville*, while the captain piloted it into position and dropped anchor. Leyte Gulf was crowded with ships. Guns roared and threw shells. Rockets crisscrossed the sky, leaving white vapor trails. Black smoke slithered up from the ground. Overhead, airplanes swarmed, screaming and shooting. In the midst of battle, a blinker message was flashed from the woods, "Welcome to our city."

MacArthur smiled and slapped Sutherland on the back, "We're here!" He climbed down a ladder to a barge that took him past a transport ship where he picked up Romulo. MacArthur hugged him, crying above the noise, "How does it feel to be home?" Quezon had died and now the new leader

Philippine president Sergio Osmena and General Carlos Romulo en route to Leyte for the Philippine liberation

of the Philippines, Sergio Osmena, rode in the flat-bottomed boat with the General and Romulo.

Fifty yards from shore, their boat ran aground. The beachmaster, who is in charge of getting people off ships in an orderly manner, growled, "Let 'em walk." MacArthur ordered the barge ramp lowered, stepped off into knee-deep water, and splashed his way to the beach near Tacloban, on the island of Leyte.

A mobile broadcasting unit was quickly set up. The General walked up to the microphone, took a deep breath, then said, "People of the Philippines, I have returned."

This historic "A-Day" landing on the island of Leyte began the liberation of the Philippines from the Japanese. From left to right, president of the Philippines Sergio Osmena, General Courtney Whitney, General Carlos Romulo, General Douglas MacArthur, General Richard Sutherland, and a CBS News correspondent.

MacArthur, with back to camera, salutes the flag at the reconquest of Corregidor.

General Douglas MacArthur, left, at his Manila headquarters in 1945

❧ NINE ❧

Rebuilding Japan

"I think the whole world was holding its breath."
—General Courtney Whitney

On July 26, 1945, the Japanese were given a choice: "Surrender or face destruction." The Japanese government failed to answer the warning. On Monday, August 6, the *Enola Gay*, a United States B-29, flew over Hiroshima and dropped an atomic bomb. On Thursday, August 9, a second atomic bomb devastated Nagasaki. MacArthur, who had thought the United States could end the war without resorting to that new bomb, said, "Japan became the victim of the most destructive weapon in the history of warfare."

Thousands of people were killed. Those who lived became ill from radiation. The city's buildings were blown apart or were burned in a fierce fire. Industry stopped. Unemployed people roamed the streets and human misery was everywhere. But more important than any of these was the people's loss of pride. On August 15, Japan surrendered.

The United States dropped atomic bombs on the cities of Hiroshima and Nagasaki. This devasting weapon destroyed both cities. Survivors suffered from severe burns and radiation.

Hiroshima, Japan, after the atomic bomb. The remains of an exposition hall and a bridge stand among the ruins of what was once a bustling city.

On September 2, 1945, United States and Japanese officials gathered aboard the battleship *Missouri*. The chaplain said a prayer and the band played the United States national anthem. Then MacArthur, commander in chief of the Southwest Pacific, appeared, walking between Admiral Chester Nimitz, commander of the Pacific Ocean areas, and Admiral William Halsey, commander of the South Pacific. The two admirals joined other officials who were standing off to the side. General MacArthur stepped up to the microphone.

A sailor whispered, "Look at Mac. Ain't he got no ribbons?" The sailor beside him answered, "If he wore them, they'd go clear over his shoulder."

MacArthur's voice was clear, "We are gathered here . . . to conclude a solemn agreement whereby peace may be restored."

Two copies of the treaty lay on the table. One treaty was for the Americans, the other for the Japanese. MacArthur motioned for the most important Japanese official to come forward. Foreign Minister Mamoru Shigemitsu hobbled toward the table, sat down, and fumbled with his hat. Then he fumbled with his gloves and cane. Halsey wanted to shout, "Sign, damn you, sign!" But MacArthur realized that the man was confused. "Sutherland!" he said. "Show him where to sign!"

As cameras clicked, MacArthur took five fountain pens from his pocket. Using all of them, he wrote his name. He handed the first pen to General Wainwright. The second pen went to Britain's General Percival. The third would be sent to West Point, the fourth to Annapolis, and the fifth was to be Jean's. After signing, MacArthur looked toward the sky and then toward Wainwright. "Where the hell are those airplanes?" he asked. Just then a swarm of B-29s and navy fighters roared across the sky. When they were gone, the General stood before a microphone. It was time for him to broadcast a message to the people of the United States. He said: "Today the guns are silent. A great tragedy has ended. A great victory has been won. The skies no longer rain death—the seas bear only commerce—men everywhere walk upright in the sunlight. . . ." It had been three years, eight months, and 22 days since Japan bombed Pearl Harbor. That day on the *Missouri*, World War II ended.

෴

On September 8 of the same year, MacArthur stepped from his car at the United States embassy in the city of Tokyo. Soldiers saluted. An honor guard presented arms. "General Eichelberger," MacArthur said, "have our country's flag unfurled." While the United States flag slid up the pole, the band played "The Star-Spangled Banner."

MacArthur had been designated supreme commander. It was his job to shape the future of Japan. He became the

The official statement of Japan's surrender was signed aboard the battleship Missouri. *Above,* Japanese foreign minister Mamoru Shigemitsu signs, and, below, MacArthur signs for the U.S.

only administrator of almost 80 million people, and he was supposed to maintain control of Japan until that country demonstrated that it was ready to become a responsible member of the family of free nations.

Jean worried about flying into Japan only a few days after its surrender. MacArthur was waiting for her at the airport. "Isn't it dangerous?" she whispered as she kissed him.

"Not at all," he told her.

He hugged his son, and the three of them headed for the New Grand Hotel. They stayed there only a few days. The United States embassy was to be their home.

Jean was unhappy with the building which had been christened "Hoover's Folly." (Hoover had been president when it was built.) Not only was the building ugly, but a bomb had gone through the roof. There was "enough water on the floor to make a wading pool," and "the furniture was ruined." Outside, rocks and trees had been split by bombs. The General said happily, "Do what you can to fix it up." Arthur, who was now seven, tugged at his mother's hand. "Do we have to live here?"

They did have to live in Japan because that was where the General's duty lay. The family had been through too much together to be separated. "We three are one," Jean said.

Every morning at 7:00 A.M., Arthur would rush into his parents' bedroom to play with his father. At the same time, a Japanese servant opened the door to four dogs. The dogs chased each other while Arthur laughed and rolled with the supreme commander. Play stopped at 8:00 A.M. when the family gathered for prayers. After his father read from the Bible, Arthur went to study his lessons.

Jean took Arthur to church every Sunday. Sometimes she attended a party, or took a trip, but she was never gone

MacArthur arrived in Japan as supreme commander. It was his job to maintain control of Japan and shape the future of that country. He governed 80 million people.

long. "Five days," she said, "is too long to be away from the General." She told a reporter, "My whole life is the General and our son, and I take care of them the best I can." When other people praised MacArthur, she'd say, "You couldn't be more right."

∽

General MacArthur was soon viewed by the Japanese as a man with unusual powers. They thought he could not only rule a country, but also cure the sick. Some called him "the new shogun." (Shoguns were military governors who once ruled Japan.) Others referred to him as "the savior of Japan." Letters from citizens poured into his office asking him to work all kinds of wonders. A Japanese journalist wrote a biography of MacArthur that spoke of him as a living god. The powerful figure of MacArthur filled a need for the defeated, hurting Japanese people.

MacArthur moved in an orderly fashion to organize the

General Douglas MacArthur poses with Japanese Emperor Hirohito. Before the 1947 Constitution was written, emperors held great power in Japan. The position is now only a ceremonial one.

country. He sent Japanese soldiers back to their families. He gave the people political and religious freedom. Torture chambers were destroyed. Political prisoners were released. Newspapers were free to publish whatever they liked. Women were allowed to vote, and the education of children was improved. For the first time, boys and girls attended the same high schools, and contract marriages ended. That meant that young men and women were free to choose their own mates instead of having their parents choose for them. Perhaps more important than any of these, a new constitution was written and elections were held. MacArthur wrote: "The constitution was probably the single most important accomplishment of the occupation. It brought to the Japanese people freedoms and privileges which they had never known. . . ."

⸺

While MacArthur was helping the Japanese people rebuild their country, trouble was brewing in Korea. Early Sunday morning, on June 25, 1950, the telephone rang in MacArthur's bedroom. He picked it up and heard, "General, the North Korean army has crossed the 38th parallel. They're swarming into South Korea!"

Communist troops crossing the 38th parallel was considered a threat to the American people because the United

After the war, Japan quickly rebuilt its cities with a hard-working and well-trained work force. Above, *construction in war-shattered Tokyo.*

States was a member of the United Nations, an organization that had promised to maintain that boundary between North and South Korea. Sixteen countries sent troops to fight the invading army. Forty-one countries sent military equipment and food. It was the beginning of another war.

MacArthur paced. "Seoul under attack! How could that happen?" He was shocked, upset, sick at heart. He didn't have to ask what had gone wrong. He knew the answer. The United States had allowed its army to become weak, and South Korea had only four divisions protecting its border. The South Koreans had been trained as peace officers, not as fighting troops. They had no air or naval forces. Although they had light weapons, they were without artillery or tanks. The Communists, on the other hand, had put artillery, tanks, and thousands of men up close to the 38th parallel.

Five years had passed since MacArthur had watched the United States flag being raised in Tokyo. Now, with 50 years of service behind him, MacArthur was facing yet another campaign. Again he confronted odds that seemed hopeless. Again there was only one way for him to understand the situation: he had to see for himself.

On a rainy morning in June, MacArthur climbed aboard his airplane, *Bataan*. He pulled out his corncob pipe, lit it, and watched the smoke curl up. The supreme commander was again planning a war. In Korea he would command troops for the United Nations.

∽ TEN ∽

The Final Years

"North Korea had struck like a cobra."
—Douglas MacArthur

The General shoved his hands in his pockets and paced the aisle of the airplane. "He's always this way," a staff officer told a reporter. "He'll walk halfway there before we set down."

Four Mustangs (P-51 fighter airplanes) flew above the *Bataan*. As MacArthur's plane passed over Suwon, a Yak (Russian airplane) dove toward it. An aide shouted, "Mayday!" Everyone ducked except MacArthur, who hurried to the window to see a Mustang peel off in chase. "We've got him cold," the General shouted.

The *Bataan* came in for a landing and bounced on the rough airstrip. Syngman Rhee, the president of Korea, greeted the General and took him to a nearby schoolhouse. "This will be your headquarters," he said.

Brigadier General Church pointed to a wall map. He carefully explained about the fighting at the border. When he finished MacArthur slapped himself on the knee and said, "Let's go up to the front and have a look."

MacArthur's jeep bumped along the winding road. Hills were steep on either side. In the valleys, streams twisted past rice paddies, scrub oak, and small firs. Holes in the ground were deep enough to hide troops. The country was perfect for guerrilla warfare.

Danger surrounded the General and his small party. A reporter wrote, "They drove through the defeated South Korean army and masses of bewildered civilian refugees. . . . Throughout the journey, the convoy risked enemy air action. . . . The crump of mortars was loud and clear. . . ."

When they arrived at their destination, MacArthur stood on a hill where he could see South Korean soldiers running away from battle. He saw ambulances filled with injured men. Shrieking missiles flew across the horizon. An

MacArthur's airplane, the Bataan, was named in honor of the brave people who fought so courageously and suffered so much. MacArthur felt so deeply about the horrors of Bataan that he would not discuss the subject.

Dr. Syngman Rhee, president of Korea, is greeted by Supreme Commander Douglas MacArthur in Tokyo. Mrs. MacArthur can be seen standing behind and to the left of President Rhee.

aide remembered that the General's sharp profile stood out against the black smoke of Seoul. His hands were in his rear pockets, and his long-stemmed pipe jutted upward.

John Muccio, the American Ambassador to Seoul, sent a wire to Tokyo. It said, "The Big Boy had a lot of guts and was magnificent." But no one knew then just how magnificent the General really was at that moment. While standing on that hill, he imagined an amphibious landing behind the North Korean lines.

〰

By September 1, 1950, the North Koreans had driven the United Nations troops back. The South Korean army was crowded into a small area around the city of Pusan. The General needed to put troops behind the North Koreans to cut the North Korean supply lines. He knew this would take an amphibious landing. Now he and his staff had to decide where this would happen. He remembered the landing he had imagined. This plan became one of MacArthur's greatest successes, but before it took place the Joint Chiefs of Staff argued about it. They did not believe his plan would work.

"The landing at Inchon will be a success," MacArthur cabled General Omar Bradley, chairman of the Joint Chiefs of Staff, in Washington, D.C.

"It won't work," Bradley answered. "It's a crazy idea—dangerous!" Bradley called President Truman, who agreed that a landing at Inchon would be a mistake.

MacArthur wanted to land his troops only 20 miles from Seoul, but many leaders in Washington thought that was too close. The North Koreans would fight hard to keep the city. MacArthur argued that he needed to be near Seoul to cut off enemy supply lines.

"The tides are too high," Bradley argued, "then too low. You won't have enough time in between high and low tide. Your ships will get stuck in the mud."

MacArthur tried to be patient. "We will time our moves carefully. Naval officers are very smart. I trust the navy."

The Joint Chiefs cautioned that mines might be in the water and that the water, which rushed in and out, would be dangerous.

Then the General told them, "We must risk the dangers unless you want our boys killed like beef in a slaughterhouse."

MacArthur won, and on Wednesday, September 13, 1950, United States destroyers and four cruisers steamed into Inchon harbor. Airplanes zoomed in overhead. While they blasted installations on the coast, 261 ships from seven different nations entered Flying Fish Channel.

When the first wave of marines landed on the beach, General MacArthur sent a message to the Joint Chiefs:

From the bridge of the *U.S.S.* Mt. McKinley, *MacArthur,* left, *watches the successful invasion of Inchon. MacArthur was commander-in-chief of the United Nations forces in Korea.*

Troops and equipment are unloaded on the beach during the invasion of Inchon, below.

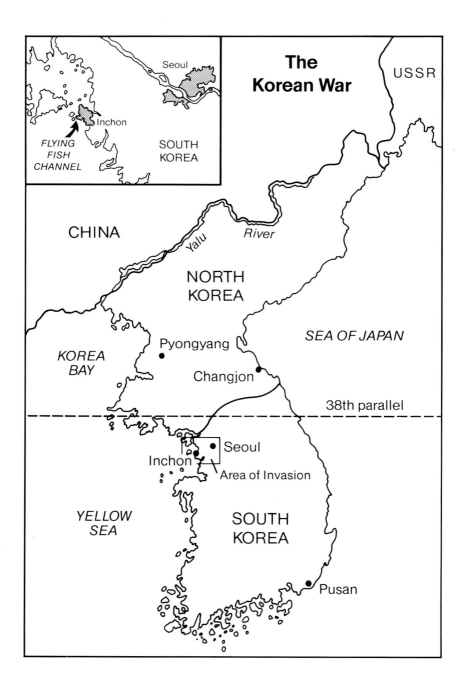

Seoul

Inchon

*FLYING
FISH
CHANNEL*

SOUTH
KOREA

**The
Korean War**

USSR

CHINA

Yalu   *River*

NORTH
KOREA

SEA OF JAPAN

*KOREA
BAY*

Pyongyang

Changjon

38th parallel

Seoul

Inchon

Area of Invasion

*YELLOW
SEA*

SOUTH
KOREA

Pusan

During a snow storm, an artillery battalion fires while on a night mission in Korea.

"First landing phase successful with losses slight. . . ." To the fleet he said, "The navy and marines have never shone more brightly than this morning."

Once again MacArthur proved himself to be one of the world's greatest generals.

∞

But then trouble followed. MacArthur believed that the United States and the United Nations had entered the war to defeat the Communists no matter what the cost. Because President Truman and the Joint Chiefs did not want war with China, they told MacArthur to hold his troops back and stay away from the Chinese border.

As the war escalated, the General felt only one weapon

Like many other areas of Korea, the village of Ko Chang, above, was almost totally destroyed by the bombing and shelling missions of the air force.

Carrying all their earthly possessions in three bundles, this Korean family approaches the demarcation line (38th parallel) between North and South Korea while a U.S. soldier watches.

President Harry Truman, right, and the Joint Chiefs of Staff disagreed with MacArthur about how to proceed in Korea.

could work well in Korea—airplanes. He ordered ninety B-29s and sent a cable that said, "We must destroy the bridges over the Yalu River to keep the Red armies from swarming across them. We must cut off their supply lines. If we don't move into China, we cannot win."

When the cable reached Washington, the plan was stopped by President Truman and the Joint Chiefs. They cabled back, "Postpone all bombing of targets within five miles of the border."

That put MacArthur's army at a disadvantage. The bridges stayed and the Chinese Communists rolled their tanks across them. They came with thousands of men and with Russian guns and ammunition. They pushed MacArthur's army back.

"Incredible!" MacArthur jerked his pipe from his mouth. "If we are not in this war to win, I will resign."

In Washington, President Truman was equally angry. "MacArthur cannot follow instructions," he stormed. "It is time to relieve him from duty." But the decision was difficult because many people thought MacArthur was a great general and they did not want him fired.

Weeks passed. MacArthur insisted that he be allowed the freedom he needed to win the war. Truman, who thought MacArthur was wrong, would not change his mind.

Finally, one day in April, 1951, Colonel Sidney Huff, an old friend and aide, telephoned Mrs. MacArthur. He wanted her to listen to a 3:00 radio broadcast because President Truman was going to say something about the General. Jean could not be reached, so Huff left word for her to return his call. Then he switched on his radio to hear, "With deep regret I have concluded that General of the Army, Douglas MacArthur, is unable to give wholehearted support to the policies of the United States and of the United Nations." As Huff sat stunned at the news, his telephone rang. It was Jean.

"Did you call, Sid?"

"Yes." He hated to tell her. "I just heard a flash over the radio from Washington saying that the General has been relieved of his command."

Moments later a cable came, signed by Omar Bradley, chairman of the Joint Chiefs. Huff delivered it to Jean. "Here it is," he said. Is there anything I can do?"

"No thanks, Sid." Her lips were tight. Her face was sad.

When Jean and the General were alone, he opened the brown army envelope. "Jeannie," he said, "we're going home at last."

∽

President Truman told the nation that he had no choice. He had acted with the deepest personal regret. But most American citizens did not believe him.

A "Punch Harry in the Nose Club" was formed in Denver,

Colorado. Workmen in Lafayette, Indiana paraded two miles through a rainstorm to a telegraph office so they could send angry telegrams to the White House. A Houston clergyman dialed Western Union to send the message, "Your removal of General MacArthur is a great victory for the Russians." Other telegrams read: IMPEACH THE IMBECILE; WE WISH TO PROTEST THE LATEST OUTRAGE ON THE PART OF THE PIG IN THE WHITE HOUSE; and IMPEACH THE RED HERRING FROM THE PRESIDENTIAL CHAIR.

Senator Richard Nixon said, "The happiest group in the country will be the Communists and their stooges.... The president has given them what they have always wanted—MacArthur's scalp." MacArthur, he said, has been "fired simply because he had the good sense and patriotism to ask that the hands of our fighting men in Korea be untied."

The Japanese people were unhappy, too. The *Nippon Times* commented that "the good wishes of 83 million Japanese people" will go with him. Jean was praised as "a symbol of wifely devotion."

On April 16, General MacArthur's motorcade left the embassy at 6:28 A.M. Almost a quarter-million Japanese people, waving small Japanese and American flags, lined the 12 miles of highway to the airport.

When the General arrived at the airport, cannons boomed a salute while 18 jet fighters and 4 superfortresses flew overhead. MacArthur said his farewells to the Japanese leaders and the diplomatic corps. Then he followed Ah Cheu, Jean, and Arthur up the ramp to the plane. At 7:20 A.M., the engines of the *Bataan* roared as the plane circled the field and headed out over the Pacific.

During their flight to Hawaii, Arthur sang to Ah Cheu

Several cities planned parades for MacArthur because many people viewed him as a hero. This parade took place in New York.

and Jean sat beside the General while he wrote the speech he would give to Congress. When the *Bataan* glided toward Hickam Field, Jean looked out of the window and saw 100,000 people down below.

"They must be there for you," Jean said to her husband.

"I hope they're not just here because they're feeling sorry for me," he said.

The people had come to meet General MacArthur because they admired him. They had planned a 20-mile parade in his honor. At the University of Hawaii campus, 3,000 students cheered as its president awarded him an honorary doctorate. "General MacArthur is one of the great Americans of this age, and in the opinion of many in this group, one of the greatest Americans of all time."

The MacArthurs said good-bye to Hawaii and then got back on the *Bataan*. When the lights from San Francisco winked into view, the General put his hand on Arthur's shoulder and said, "Well, my boy, we're home."

When MacArthur stepped out on the plane's ramp, his gold-trimmed cap and his trench coat were bathed in spotlights. A band played. Cannons fired. Ten thousand San Franciscans broke through police lines to gather around the General's airplane. That was only the beginning. The MacArthurs' motorcade crawled through the streets where a half-million people cheered. The following morning the MacArthurs rode in a parade. Hundreds of people threw confetti, ticker tape, and feathers from pillows.

When they arrived at the airport in Washington, D.C., 12,000 people were there to greet him. The Joint Chiefs of Staff were there. They brought him a silver tea service as a gift. The secretary of defense was there. But Harry Truman was absent. The crowd pushed past barriers and swept the official greeters aside. For a few moments Jean and Arthur were separated by the excited people who pushed and shoved. Some were knocked to the ground. The only people who managed well were the Washington reporters who wore football helmets.

∽

The next day MacArthur addressed the political leaders in Washington. When Jean entered the visitor's gallery at 12:13 P.M., the audience clapped. At 12:18, Arthur was escorted to the well of the house. At 12:20 the floodlights were turned on and the senators marched in. The room was quiet—tense. Then, at 12:31, the doorkeeper cried: "Mr. Speaker, General of the Army, Douglas MacArthur!" The

Douglas MacArthur closed his illustrious military career with an address to Congress. In his speech, he remarked that "Old soldiers never die. They just fade away..."

audience jumped to its feet, shouting, clapping, and pounding on desks. MacArthur, standing tall, strode down the aisle.

The General told of the war in Asia. He praised America's "fighting sons." He said, "I am closing my 52 years of military service.... The world has turned over many times since I took the oath on the Plain at West Point, and the hopes and dreams have long since vanished. But I still remember the refrain of one of the most popular barrack ballads of that day, ... 'Old soldiers never die. They just fade away....' I now close my military career and just fade away — an old soldier who tried to do his duty as God gave him the light to see that duty." He stopped, waited a minute, then whispered, "Good-bye." He handed his manuscript to the clerk and left the chambers to begin life as a private citizen.

EPILOGUE

General Douglas MacArthur could not just fade away. He was a hero to millions of Americans. The General said afterward, "America took me to its heart with a roar that will never leave my ears."

MacArthur stormed the country giving rousing political speeches. In Houston, Texas, a half-million people welcomed him; 20,000 packed Dewey Square in Boston; and 300,000 applauded him in Seattle. After riding in a motorcade behind a hundred policemen on motorcycles, MacArthur spoke to 50,000 people at Soldier Field in Chicago.

The MacArthurs lived at the Waldorf Towers in New York, where they leased a suite for $450 a month. The usual price was $133 a day. Railroads and airlines gave him presidential treatment, and, although the General said he was not interested in politics, there was a wave of enthusiasm across the country to elect him president of the United States.

But MacArthur did not receive the nomination for the presidency. He enjoyed civilian life. "I find the liberties of private life refreshing and exhilarating," he said. He became board chairman of Remington Rand and commuted two or three times a week from New York to the company's offices in Stratford, Connecticut.

Jean browsed the shops in New York, and Arthur attended school there. He graduated from Columbia University in 1961. The General insisted that he approved of his son remaining a civilian. "My mother put too much pressure on me," he said. "Being number one is the loneliest job in the world, and I wouldn't wish it on any son of mine."

Eventually, Arthur moved to the West Side of Manhattan and changed his name to conceal his identity. His music is the most important thing to him.

MacArthur died in New York at Walter Reed Hospital on Sunday, April 5, 1964. He was 84 years old. The General had drawn up specific plans for his funeral that were un-characteristically modest. He wanted to be buried in a plain, gray steel, government-issue casket. He wore twin circlets of stars, but no ribbons or medals on his breast, as he had instructed.

On Monday, 2500 men from West Point gathered on the plain and saluted as six cannons roared. On Tuesday, 35,000 New Yorkers waited in line to pass by his coffin. At 8:00 A.M. on Wednesday, a senior cadet commanded the start of the funeral procession with a crisp "Forward march!" The West Point band was followed by a battalion of cadets and an honor guard of generals and admirals. Close behind was the caisson, carrying the coffin and drawn by six Fort Myer horses.

MacArthur was buried in the MacArthur Memorial in Norfolk, Virginia. When Jean dies, she will be buried there also.

Every year hundreds of admiring Americans visit the MacArthur Memorial to pay their respects to one of America's great heroes.

A West Point cadet commanded the start of MacArthur's funeral procession. The caisson carrying the coffin was drawn by six horses from Fort Myer.

Appendix

Rank (grade) for officers of the U.S. Army

The rank, or grade, system indicates a person's authority and standing in the military. The number of stars on an officer's uniform shows his or her rank. The rank of officers is:

Brigadier General . . . . one star ☆

Major General . . . . two stars ☆☆

Lieutenant General . . . . three stars ☆☆☆

General . . . . four stars ☆☆☆☆

General of the Army . . . . five stars ☆☆☆☆☆

Chief of Staff

A Chief of Staff is a senior officer of the U.S. Army or Air Force. He or she is a member of the Joint Chiefs of Staff.

Joint Chiefs of Staff

The Joint Chiefs of Staff are military advisers to the president of the United States, the secretary of defense, and the National Security Council. They include a chairman, the chiefs of staff of the army, the air force, and the navy. When marine corps matters are considered, the commandant of the marine corps is included. The chairman is appointed by the president and approved by the Senate.

Allies During World War II

Australia
Belgium
Canada
China
Czechoslovakia
Denmark
Ethiopia

France
Great Britain
Greece
India
Netherlands
New Zealand

Norway
Poland
South Africa
Soviet Union
United States
Yugoslavia

Many other countries declared war against the Axis and can be called Allies. The Allies listed above either fought against the Axis with large conventional forces or underground resistance movements, or were occupied by Axis armies.

The Axis

Bulgaria
Finland
Germany

Hungary
Italy

Japan
Romania

GLOSSARY

A-Day: the day that Pacific forces landed on the island of Leyte to begin liberation of the Philippines

Allies: in World War I, nations united against the Central European powers; in World War II, nations united against the Axis powers

amphibious landing: coordinated action of land, sea, and air forces organized for invasion

armistice: an agreement to stop fighting for a long period of time. An armistice often leads to a peace treaty, as the armistice that ended World War I did.

Axis: nations united against the Allied powers in World War II; the three main Axis powers were Germany, Italy, and Japan.

B-17: bomber plane nicknamed the Flying Fortress

B-29: most advanced bomber used in World War II; nicknamed the Superfortress

Bataan: peninsula on the island of Luzon in the Philippines, on the west side of Manila Bay

battalion: a large body of troops organized to act together

Bonus March: demonstration by veterans during the Great Depression to persuade Congress to pass legislation that would provide payment of promised bonuses

cavalrymen: soldiers mounted on horseback or moving in motor vehicles and assigned to missions that require mobility

Civilian Conservation Corps: a program established by Congress in 1933 as part of the New Deal. Its purpose was to provide young men with useful work and vocational training.

convoy: protective escort

doughboy: name given to infantry soldiers, especially during World War I

dugout: protective shelter dug in the ground

Great Depression: a period in the 1930s marked by unemployment, business failures, and poverty. The Great Depression followed the stock market crash of 1929 and lasted until 1941, when the U.S. entered World War II.

guerrilla: a person who is part of a unit that engages in irregular warfare involving harassment and sabotage

infantry: soldiers trained to fight on foot

leapfrogging: to progress as if in a game of leapfrog in which one player vaults over another; one military unit advancing around or over another

malaria: disease that is transmitted by certain mosquitoes and is characterized by fever and chills

no-man's land: name given to the battlefields between the two front lines during World War I

open city: city that is not defended or occupied by military troops and therefore, by international law, should not be bombarded by enemy forces

P-51: fighter plane called the Mustang and used in World War II

PT boat: fast, light craft that is armed with torpedoes

Rainbow Division: U.S. Army division formed from National Guard units from several states during World War II; 42nd Division

ration: to distribute equitably, usually sparingly

United Nations: an organization of 159 nations that works for world peace and security and the betterment of humanity. Each nation sends representatives to the UN headquarters in New York City, where they discuss world problems.

For Further Reading

Dupuy, Trevor Nevitt and Julia Crick. *The Military History of World War I*. 12 vol. New York: Franklin Watts, 1967.

Egeberg, Roger Olaf, M.D. *The General*. New York: Hippocrene Books, 1983.

Fincher, E. B. *The War in Korea*. New York: Franklin Watts, 1981.

James, D. Clayton. *The Years of MacArthur*. Boston: Houghton Mifflin Company, 1985.

Lawson, Don. *The United States in World War II*. New York: Abelard-Schuman, 1963.

MacArthur, Douglas. *Reminiscences*. New York: McGraw-Hill Book Co., 1964.

Manchester, William. *American Caesar, Douglas MacArthur 1880-1964*. Boston: Little, Brown and Company, 1978.

Mayer, S. L. *MacArthur*. Northbrook, Illinois: Book Value International, Inc., 1981.

Skipper, G. C. *MacArthur and the Philippines*. Chicago: Children's Press, 1982.

Steinberg, Alfred. *Douglas MacArthur*. New York: G. P. Putnam's Sons, 1961.

Sweeney, James B. *Army Leaders of World War II*. New York: Franklin Watts, 1984.

Acknowledgments

The illustrations are reproduced through the courtesy of: the MacArthur Memorial, pp. 6, 9 (all), 13 (both), 18, 31, 32 (bottom), 36, 39, 40, 43, 52, 56, 68 (both), 76, 77, 78 (both), 83 (bottom), 85, 86, 90, 100, 105; Archives Division, Texas State Library, p. 14; the United States Military Academy Archives, pp. 17, 32 (top), 70; the Library of Congress, pp. 22, 55, 83, 97, 102; the National Archives, pp. 26 (both), 45, 46 (all), 73 (both), 80, 81, 87, 93 (bottom); the United States Army, pp. 71, 91, 95, 96 (both); the United States Navy, p.93 (top left); Philippines Tourism Office, p. 61.
Maps on pages 28, 58, 74-75, and 94 are by Laura Westlund.

INDEX